COOL SPORTS

Skateboarding

Aaron Carr

MEDIA ENHANCED BOOKS
AV2 BY WEIGL
ADDED VALUE • AUDIO VISUAL

www.av2books.com

AV² provides enriched content that supplements and complements this book. Weigl's AV² books strive to create inspired learning and engage young minds in a total learning experience.

Go to **www.av2books.com**, and enter this book's unique code.

BOOK CODE

M430793

AV² by Weigl brings you media enhanced books that support active learning.

Your AV² Media Enhanced books come alive with...

Audio
Listen to sections of the book read aloud.

Video
Watch informative video clips.

Embedded Weblinks
Gain additional information for research.

Try This!
Complete activities and hands-on experiments.

Key Words
Study vocabulary, and complete a matching word activity.

Quizzes
Test your knowledge.

Slide Show
View images and captions, and prepare a presentation.

... and much, much more!

Published by AV² by Weigl
350 5th Avenue, 59th Floor New York, NY 10118
Website: www.av2books.com   www.weigl.com

Library of Congress Cataloguing in Publication data available upon request.
Fax 1-866-449-3445 for the attention of the Publishing Records department.

ISBN 978-1-61913-512-3 (hard cover)
ISBN 978-1-61913-518-5 (soft cover)

Printed in the United States of America in North Mankato, Minnesota
4 5 6 7 8 9 17 16 15 14 13

042013
WEP170413

Editor: Aaron Carr   Art Director: Terry Paulhus

Weigl acknowledges Getty Images as the primary image supplier for this title.

COOL SPORTS

Skateboarding

CONTENTS

Skateboarding is a sport.
Some people skateboard
just to have fun.
Others like to do tricks
and jumps.

A skateboard is a board with four wheels. Most skateboards bend up at each end.

Like a PRO

Pro skaters do tricks with their skateboards.

7

Skaters should always wear a helmet. Helmets keep skaters safe when they fall.

Pro skaters wear
helmets and
knee pads.

People can ride skateboards in many places. Some people ride on sidewalks. Other people go to skateparks.

Like a PRO

Pro skaters ride in many kinds of skateparks.

It is important for people to practice. This helps them become good skaters.

Like a PRO

Pro skaters must practice for many hours every day.

Skaters go down a large ramp and jump over a big gap. This is called Big Air.

Like a PRO

Pro skaters get points for doing tricks in Big Air.

Skaters ride in a U-shaped ramp and do tricks. This is called Vert.

Like a PRO

Pro skaters must land many tricks.

Skaters ride through a park jumping over stairs, rails, and other things. This is called Street.

Like a PRO

Pro skaters use all of the things in a Street park.

Great skaters come from all around the world to compete in the X Games.

People come to watch the skaters do big jumps and tricks.

SKATEBOARDING FACTS

These pages provide detailed information that expands on the interesting facts found in this book. These pages are intended to be used by adults as a learning support to help young readers round out their knowledge of each sport in the *Cool Sports* series.

Pages 4–5

Skateboarding was created in the 1950s by two surfers in California. They wanted to practice their skills when away from water. In 1978, Alan "Ollie" Gelfand changed the way people use skateboards. He invented a way to launch himself and his board into the air without using his hands. This trick became known as an ollie.

Pages 6–7

Skateboards are often made of maple wood. Common boards used in competition curve upward at both ends. This allows skaters to perform jumps and tricks without their feet slipping off the board. Skateboards have four rubber wheels. Metal pieces called trucks attach the wheels to the board.

Pages 8–9

The helmet is the most important piece of safety equipment. Helmets have saved many skaters from serious injuries. Most skaters also wear knee pads and elbow pads. Skaters can break their wrists if they fall on their hands. Instead, they learn how to use their knee pads and elbow pads to cushion a fall.

Pages 10–11

Skateboarding can be done almost anywhere. Sidewalks and empty parking lots are perfect for skaters who want to explore. They can ride walls, curbs, and ledges. Skateparks are special areas made for skateboarding. They often have ramps and jumps. Many skateparks include railings, halfpipes, and other obstacles.

**Pages
12–13**

Practice is the most important part of becoming good at any sport. Most professional skaters practice for many hours every day. They push themselves to try new tricks and explore new places. By doing this, skaters find obstacles they have never tried before. This forces them to try new moves and improve their skills.

**Pages
14–15**

Big Air involves skateboarding down an 80-foot (24-meter) ramp and launching over a 70-foot (21-m) gap. The skater then rides up a 27-foot (8-m) quarterpipe. At the top, the skater shoots into the air and performs a variety of tricks before landing. Danny Way set a record for the longest jump, at 79 feet (24 m), in the Big Air event.

**Pages
16–17**

Vert competitions take place on a 120-foot (37-m) wide, 11-foot (3-m) high halfpipe. Skaters ride from the top of one side of the halfpipe to the top of the other side in a continuous motion. At each side, skaters launch into the air and perform tricks. They only get 45 seconds to do their tricks. Tricks are scored for difficulty and variety.

**Pages
18–19**

Street skaters compete in a skatepark made up of ramps, stairs, rails, ledges, boxes, and other obstacles. Each skater takes three timed runs through the park. They can use any of the park's obstacles as many times as they want. Skaters are judged on style, difficulty, variety, originality, and number of tricks performed.

**Pages
20–21**

The X Games is an annual sports tournament that showcases the best athletes in extreme sports. The X Games started in 1995. It includes events for skateboarding, BMX, moto X, inline skating, street luge, sky surfing, and rock climbing. The X Games attract the best extreme athletes from around the world each year.

KEY WORDS

Research has shown that as much as 65 percent of all written material published in English is made up of 300 words. These 300 words cannot be taught using pictures or learned by sounding them out. They must be recognized by sight. This book contains 60 common sight words to help young readers improve their reading fluency and comprehension. This book also teaches young readers several important content words. These words are paired with pictures to aid in learning and improve understanding.

Page	Sight Words First Appearance
4	a, and, do, have, is, just, like, others, people, some, to
6	at, each, end, four, most, up, with
7	their
8	always, keep, should, they, when
10	can, go, in, many, on, places
11	kinds, of, use
12	for, good, helps, important, it, them, this
13	day, every, must
14	down, large, over
15	get, points
17	land
18	things, through
19	all, the
20	around, big, come, from, great, watch, world

Page	Content Words First Appearance
4	fun, jumps, Skateboarding, sport, tricks
6	board, skateboards, wheels
7	pro, skaters
8	helmet
9	knee pads
10	sidewalks, skateparks
13	hours
14	Big Air, gap, ramp
16	Vert
18	park, rails, stairs, Street
20	X Games

www.av2books.com